Art Never Comes First

Verses of Silence and Sorrows

Bishal Raj Biswas

BookLeaf Publishing

India | USA | UK

Made with ❤ on the BookLeaf Publishing Platform
www.bookleafpub.in
www.bookleafpub.com

About the Author

Bishal Raj Biswas is a 23-year-old poet and educator from Malbazar, West Bengal. Holding a Master's degree in English Literature, he is deeply drawn to allegory, philosophy, and the beauty of tragedy. Currently working as a teacher, he continues to nurture his passion for learning and research. Having qualified for the UGC NET for Ph.D. , he strives for greater achievements before fully stepping into academia. Throughout his academic journey, he has won multiple prizes in extempore, quizzes, and essay writing at the university level. Beyond his literary pursuits, he is an avid fan of anime and football, drawing creative inspiration from both.

Dedication

To you,

For being my pole star, my guiding light, and my source of euphoria on days when I felt like I couldn't go on. During the gloomy, overcast days, you were the umbrella that shielded me from the downpour, the very epitome of grace. You were the bright light that pulled me from the darkest abyss, bringing incandescence, like the Aurora Borealis illuminating a frozen, barren landscape covered in eternal ice. For restoring vitality to my work, I shall forever be grateful.

Acknowledgement

Writing a book is definitely not a piece of cake. With that in mind, I'd like to express my heartfelt gratitude to those who played a crucial role in my life and helped me achieve one of my childhood dreams. Thank you, Mummy and Papa, without your unconditional support, this book never would have come to be. I am especially grateful to my mother, Mrs. Swapna Biswas, who constantly nagged me and scolded me every time I made a mistake. It was her discipline that pushed me towards the right path and prevented me from falling into traps. I am also deeply thankful to my father, Mr. Bipul Kanti Biswas, for always saying yes to my demands. While I rarely asked for things, whenever I truly needed something in my childhood, it was your hard work that provided for me.

A special thanks to my dear sisters, Priyanka Biswas and Akansha Biswas. Didivai, you always looked after me and supported me like a mother nurtures her child. Monu, our relationship has always been like that of a snake and a mongoose, constantly at odds, but if anyone ever dared to mess with me, no one would be worse for them than you. Much love to my dear nephew, Ayush Sarkar, my biggest supporter who has always cheered me on in all my ventures. I'd also like to thank my brother-in-law, Mr. Nandan Sarkar, who paved the way for me to pursue my Master's degree by sharing his wisdom and experiences. Bondidi and Didun, much love to you too.

None of this would have been possible without Miss Protyusha Sen, who has always been my source of motivation and encouragement. You inspire me every day with your patience and thoughtfulness. You stood by my side with kindness and compassion even on days when I was insufferable because of the turbulence in my life, and for that, I am truly grateful.

For the sake of brevity, I would like to acknowledge and thank those who had the greatest impact on the completion of this book, especially my childhood friend, Arnab Paul, whose innovative ideas and creative inputs over two cups of tea at local tea stalls kept me inspired amidst the chaos of life. I am also grateful to him for helping me design the front cover page of my book, bringing my vision to life with his creativity and effort.

I would also like to extend my gratitude to Arpita Das Gupta Ma'am, who sowed the seeds of curiosity in me through her intriguing literature lectures during my graduation. Additionally, thanks to Basudev Paul Sir for his engaging discussions on poetry, which I deeply cherished.

Last but certainly not least, I am most grateful to myself, for not giving up on this process and for continuing this journey with pure perseverance and utmost dedication.

"What horrifies me most is the idea of being useless : well-educated, brilliantly promising, and fading out into an indifferent middle age."

— Sylvia Plath

"Do not go gentle into that good night.
Rage, rage against the dying of the light."

— Dylan Thomas

"Poetry is the spontaneous overflow of powerful feelings: it takes its origin from emotion recollected in tranquility."

— William Wordsworth

Preface

Dear Reader,

In a world that constantly shifts, where many still believe that expressing emotions or vulnerabilities diminishes a man's strength, I stand in defiance. Strength is not found in silence but in the courage to voice our struggles. Every soul with a muse holds the power to rise above setbacks, whether financial, emotional, or social as long as that muse serves as a beacon of motivation and encouragement. Even in despair, a true muse ignites the spirit, enabling one to rise from the ashes like a phoenix. This collection delves into contemporary struggles such as stress, societal pressure, the silent burden of mental health, and even the heartache of witnessing nature suffer under the weight of global warming. But above all, it speaks of something many hesitate to acknowledge: mental depression. It is a reality people often endure in silence, yet it is just as significant as any physical ailment, deserving of attention, care, and open conversation. Depression does not discriminate. It manifests in countless forms, a heartbreak that leaves one hollow, an endless job that drains the soul, the anxiety of unemployment, the crushing weight of overwork, or the suffocating fear of missing out. From teenagers to young adults to middle-aged individuals, everyone carries a burden, often unseen, often unspoken. But by vocalizing our pain, we reclaim our strength. Within these pages, you will find reflections on suffering, adversity, grief, anxiety, and loss. There are odes to a rising football player, moments of quiet self-reflection, and an advisory poem inspired by the art of anime. This book also contains a deeply personal poem dedicated to my mother, who was diagnosed with lupus, a rare autoimmune disease where the body's own immune system turns against itself, attacking healthy tissues and organs. It is an unpredictable and relentless condition, bringing pain, fatigue, and complications that shadow everyday life. Despite this, my mother continues to fight with unwavering strength, refusing to let her illness define her. This poem is a tribute to her resilience, a testament to her perseverance, and above all, a prayer that she remains well. Additionally, this collection includes "Ode to an Old Friend" and "Jorethang Rockstar," two poems dedicated to two remarkable friends I've made over time. With them, I share a bond that feels like brotherhood, built on trust, laughter, and countless cherished memories. These poems are an ode to friendship, the kind that stands firm through the passage of time. This book also holds a deeply personal loss, the passing of my beloved baby cats, Kohaku and Midori, who now live on through the two poems dedicated to them. Life is not a perfectly arranged string of lights, nor a radiant halo of perpetual joy. It is a mosaic of fragmented moments, each piece shaped by sorrow, resilience, and hope. This collection is born from countless sleepless nights, each poem a whisper of pain and perseverance. I invite you to walk this journey with me where silence

and sorrow intertwine, and beauty rises from
the ashes of struggle.

Index

Ode to Mental Health

No one speaks of the silent weight,
the burden carried in the mind,
unseen, unheard, yet heavy
as a body bruised and broken.

When someone dares to voice their pain,
they are silenced,
"It's all in your head," they say,
"Smile, move on, be strong."

Yes, it is in the mind,
but wounds of the soul cut just as deep.
A broken bone is tended with care,
but what of a spirit unraveling,
a heart lost in the fog of despair?

Left untreated, a wound festers.
Left unspoken, pain expands,
turning days restless,
turning nights into battles
with shadows that never sleep.

Without a healthy mind,
the body falters,
like a traveler forced to walk forever
without rest, without pause.

How can a child be expected to thrive,
when their world is crumbling?
How can anyone give their best,
when the weight of existence is too much to
bear?

Let there be no shame in seeking light.
Let the unseen wounds be acknowledged,
spoken, healed.
For mental health is not a whisper to be
ignored,
but a truth that must be heard.

Young Adults

Young adults, caught in between,
too old to dream, too young to lead.
They reach for the world, eager and bold,
but hands pull them back "Not yet, not now."

They crave to wander, to chase the sky,
to lose themselves, to learn, to try.
Yet they are children when they dare to
explore,
but adults when they falter, judged for
evermore.

They are expected to be responsible, but
never free.
Expected to follow rules, but never make
their own.
Their joys are called childish, their struggles, a
phase.
"Grow up," they say, yet when they do, the
world refuses.

Their Desires are dismissed, voices are
silenced,
Dreams are locked tight behind a red door.
To feel, to fall, to hope, to yearn,
is met with scorn instead of concern.

Is it any wonder they fall silent?
That the weight of expectation
settles like a stone in their chest?
Trapped between what they are
and what the world demands them to be.

Let them breathe, let them be,
let them stumble, let them see.
For in their laughter, in their flight,
lies the ember of their light.

The Samsa Syndrome

Adults suffer in silence,
their pain hidden beneath tired smiles.
When life strikes with all its weight,
yet they remain standing,
With their hands calloused from holding on.

Bills pile up like unanswered prayers,
dreams shrink beneath the weight of survival.
"Find a better job," they hear,
as if they are not already searching,
as if they do not lie awake at night,
mapping out a way forward.

At some point, we wonder,
is every working man Gregor Samsa,
waking up each morning
to a life that no longer feels his own?

They swallow their grief,
push through exhaustion,
return to work like clockwork machines,
not for themselves,
but for the ones they love.

And in return, they ask for so little,
Just a kind word, or a slight touch of warmth,
something to remind them
they are more than just labor,
more than just survival.

The Forgotten Ones

Parents labor in silence,
hands weathered by years of toil,
working endlessly to provide,
while their children, far away,
live lives of pretense.

In bustling cities,
their calls go unanswered,
"Just studying for exams,"
they say,
yet nights are spent in endless parties,
dancing under lights that blind the truth.

Back home, in small towns,
the parents wait,
expecting nothing but a simple hello,
but the distance between them grows,
not measured in miles,
but in lies whispered through silence.

The children, wrapped in their illusions,
spend without care,
while parents work 24 hours
to earn a fraction of what is lost in a night,
unaware that the money they throw away
is the result of another's sacrifice.

The world turns,
and the generation of today
clings to fleeting moments of joy,
forgetting that true worth is in the hands
that held them,
the ones who carried them through life,
not the friends who vanish when the money
runs out.

One day, the parties will end,
the crowd will disperse,
and it will be family,
those forgotten ones,
who will be there to pick up the pieces.

So open your eyes,
and see the cost of your choices.
Honour the ones who gave everything
so you could be who you are.
Fix yourself,
before it's too late,
and realize that love was never in the clubs,
but in the home you left behind.

Quiet Moments

I long to transcend this material world,
to escape the weight of its ephemeral desires
and endless demands. There's a pull,
deep within, towards something beyond the
tangible, something eternal.

Yet, I find myself tied to the routines,
The needs, and the frailty of this existence.
My spirit yearns to soar,
but the gravity of life holds me down.

In the quiet moments, I sense the sublime,
just out of reach, but my hands remain full
of
the mundane. The struggle between
transcendence and my reality thus lingers...

Sinking Ship

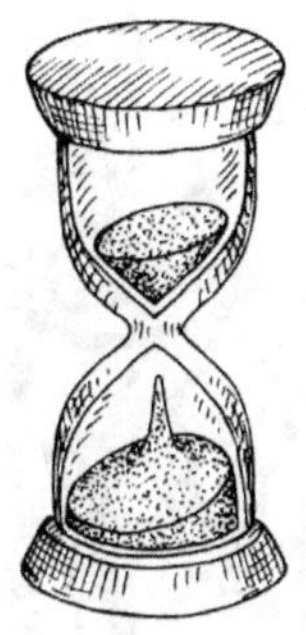

I've got an hourglass, time slipping away,
Just 15 days left to keep the storm at bay.
A ship that's sinking, I'm caught in between
Do I fight the waves or leave the unseen?

To sink while trying, giving it my all,
Or walk away before I fall?
The clock keeps ticking, the sands unwind,
What path to take? I'm torn in mind.

But whether I stay or let it go,
Only time and courage will let me know.

Game or Love

What is a game but never played?
Is love a name, by which one is slayed?
Was it his naivety or his sobriety
that had been the root cause of all his anxiety.

Is love alive? Does she breathe?
Or is she dead and gone and buried.
Was it her culpability or her ethical dilemma
that had been the cause of all the trauma!

Was it love that killed the stoic?
Or was it his own gullibility,
for believing, a skeptic would be immune
from experiencing the charms of the mortal
realm
Despaired and dreary lied his remains,
Little did he know it pours when it rains.

Obnoxious at Thirteen

A sparrow in slumber stood on a branch
elapsing his days on a monotonous trance
As the days passed by, solitarily he wondered,
obnoxious at thirteen yet passionate with
elegance,

Every beast looked up towards him
with eyes filled with envy and covetousness
yet the sparrow remained carefree in his own
domain
celebrating his freedom to fly high in the sky

Amidst the forest lied a serpent,
with a mind filled with depravity,
the charlatan would often sway
the horde of beasts into lunacy.

The Sparrow and the Serpent
would often gaze at one another
Unaware that both, in their own disguise,
Envied the other's life through veiled, wistful
eyes.

Farewell to Kohaku

Kohaku, my gentle friend, you're gone,
A light has extinguished by the dawn.
I fought for you, I tried so much,
Fed you milk, with my tender touch.

Through illness, I stood by your side,
My love for you, it never died.
I cleaned, I cared, I prayed, I fought,
But destiny had other thoughts.

Your body stiff, your strength betrayed,
Yet in your eyes, resolve had stayed.
With fading breath, you tried to rise,
To ease my heart with one last try.

As nature cradled her gentle guest.
Beneath the sun, you lied and rested,
Your last breathe was not cruel
Yet my grief feels like an endless storm

To hold your body, cold and bereft of life
left my arms heavy and my mind numb
But Kohaku, now, my only plea remains
That you are free and shall flee in the heavens
above.

May peace surround your lively soul,
In the fields of light, may you meet with
kittens alike
Om Shanti, my prayer to the heavens,
Farewell, my Kohaku, till we reunite.

They Lied

They lied when they said a cat has nine lives,
They lied when they claimed it's just an
animal.
But they weren't lying when they softly
whispered
"Don't get too attached, you'll only lose your
heart as its heart stops beating."

They lied when they said love is just for
humans
They lied when they promised "you'll love
again."

They lied when they claimed the pain would
subside,
But they weren't lying when they said it feels
like you've died.

They lied when they said time heals all
wounds,
They lied when they swore memories are not
forever
They lied when they said strength is achieved
through adversity,
But they weren't lying when they said grief
burdens the mind.

They lied when they said, "It's not worth the
tears,"
They lied when they mocked your deepest
fears.
They lied when they vowed you'd easily part,
But they weren't lying when they said it
would break your heart.

Euphoria

Students will come, and students will go,
Teachers will teach, and teachers will guide
Yet the classroom will stand, with patience
and grace,
Witness to countless laughter, to bittersweet
memories that time won't erase.

Desks and benches, carved with names,
Walls that whispers, love's untold tales
A second home, where hearts would meet,
Where lessons are learnt, both bitter and
sweet.

Lunch breaks filled with endless cheer,
Short walks stretching far and near.
Round in circles, on the ground we'd sit,
Singing and laughing, never to quit.

Antakshari tunes and dumb charades were
played,
Names were matched for compatibility in
flames.
A carefree world, where time stood still,
Unaware of life's coming uphill.

For though we leave, the walls remain,
Echoing voices of joy and pain.
Names just remained as contacts in phones,
promises to keep in touch, now overthrown.

The Anime Rules

Dear reader, never go on a coffee date with a
crush,
Learn the lesson from Ken Kaneki's hush.
Tokyo might have a human, not a ghoul,
If he had known love's painful rule.

Dear reader, don't chase a girl who doesn't
care,
Don't be like Naruto, caught in despair.
Look for your Hinata, who sees only you,
A love so pure, unwavering and true.

Dear reader, Don't be oblivious like Jon Snow,
Sacrificing love for the greater good.
Instead, be like Obito, fierce and strong,
Fighting for Rin, until death takes you apart.

Dear reader, love her while she's still alive
Observe her actions, let your heart be your
guide
Don't be an innocent fool, unaware of the
signs,
Like Arima Kosei, remained blind to Kaori's
subtle lines.

Ode to a Night

The mornings are tough, they bring routine,
A checklist to follow, the day so keen.
The afternoons are warm, but anxiety grows,
As time ticks away, and pressure shows.

The evenings are soothing, with a gentle call,
But people expect you to give it your all.
They want your company, your laughter, your
cheer,
But it's the night that holds what's dear.

For in the night, when the world is still,
I do what I love, with time to fill.
I watch my favorite show, where the heroes
rise and die,
Or an anime fight, where the protagonist
levels up and flies

I grab some popcorn, settle in tight,
As Chelsea plays with all their might.
The world sleeps on, but I'm wide awake,
In the quiet night, my mind is comforted.

While morning is calm, and afternoon a
break,
Evenings are for moments with friends and
mates to partake.
But it's the night, which is so full and true,
That gives me time, to just be me, and renew.

Ode to Cole Palmer

We are the Blues, we have won it all,
Yet 2022 showed the true colours of real
Chelsea fans' call.
The Post Tuchel era brought anxiety and
sleepless nights,
Watching our beloved side fall into dreadful
sights.

At times, the world laughed and pointed at
us,
But we stood strong, no matter the fuss.
While others switched for glory, we stayed
true,
Supporting you through the darkest of blue.

Managers came, and managers went,
Players bought and sold with no end.
But still, the results failed to shine,
Until we found a light so divine.

Then came Cole Palmer, a beacon so bright,
In the midst of our struggle, he reignited our
fight.
From the abyss, he brought us to grace,
With assists and goals, a steady pace.

This is for our modern savior, ice-cold and
wise,
Cole Palmer, you've shown us how to rise.

Ode to Malbazar

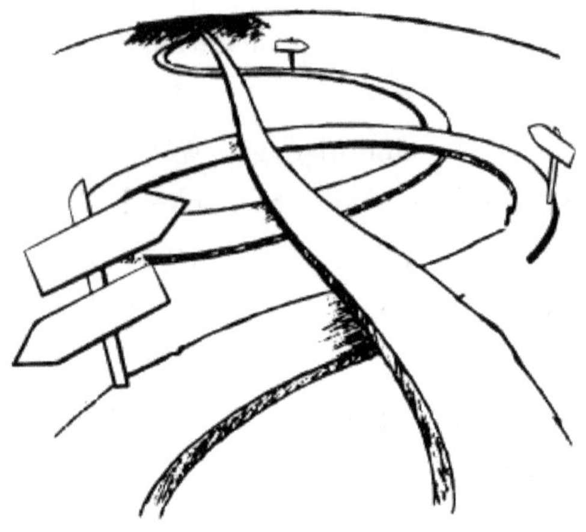

Malbazar, is not just a place, its a home,
Where pristine rivers flow and kind winds
blow
Nestled deep in the heart of the Duars,
Crowned with hills across and kissed by stars
above.

Here, tea gardens stretch like emerald seas,
and folks are seen moving slowly in the
morning breeze.

The rivers Murti and Neora flows through its
vicinity,
Where the clock stops beating, and passersby
stand still.

Beyond its heart, as the horizons stretch, the
hills arise
Samsing's chilled altitude and Gorubathan's
clear blue skies.
Where the mist wraps the cold abodes in its
embrace,
A haven carved with nature's full fledged
grace.

Kolkata beats with West Bengal's pride,
But here, the countryside resides.
Where Siliguri's city life may shine so bright,
Yet Malbazar glows with softer countryside
vibe.

A small town where all are known,
Bound by love, by roots, by stone.
The Hanuman temple, sacred and bright,
A beacon of faith, which draws souls from
places afar to its light.

As the clock tower strikes six,
residents of the town have their snacks and
tea.
As monsoons drape the earth in rain,
Bittersweet memories of the past are revived
again.

Winters chill with icy breath,
Summers pass in tempered depth.
Yet when the rains begin to start,
They paint the town upon my heart.

Oh, Malbazar, so warm, so free,
A town with limited opportunities, but
infinite tranquility
Oh, Malbazar, so warm, so free,
A town of people with dreams, a home to me.

Ode to Saraswati Puja

The morning of Vasant Panchami begins
early,
with the rustle of new clothes and soft
murmurs of prayer.
Children rise, bathed in the gentle chill of the
dawn,
their eyes set on the day of devotion
offering prayers to Ma Saraswati,
goddess of knowledge, art, and wisdom.

The trees wear blossoms of palash,
a silent signal that Vasant Panchami is near
when palash blooms on the trees, some of the
flowers fall and cover the path beneath,
they whisper of the festival's imminent
arrival.

The streets come alive,
With abundance of clashing Colours
complementing one another
With boys in contrasting kurtas, girls in
radiant sarees,
Intermingling and blending into a vibrant
kaleidoscope of youth and tradition.

No Roses presented or confessions whispered.
Just the laughter of the companions echoing
through the open air,
With the bunch of friends walking together,
hopping from one pandal to the next,
where moments of shared affection and
unspoken love unfold.

It is the month of February, Vasant Panchami
is here,
and for one day, the world is a canvas
a poem painted in hues of yellow and white.

Ode to an Old Friend

We don't talk every day,
don't meet too often,
never cared to take a picture.
But when one of us stumbles,
the other is always there.

No grand plans, no fancy places,
just two cups of tea at a roadside stall,
talking about sports, politics, the world,
never wasting time on gossip.

We don't call each other best friends,
don't make loud claims,
because in friendship, words mean less than
action.
Loyalty is quiet, but it stands tall.

A 10 rupees tea, a 10 miles ride,
worth more than any expensive café.
Because peace matters more than luxury,
and real bonds don't need a spotlight.

We don't glorify what we have,
don't speak praises to others.
But when one of us is absent,
the other stands guard against unkind words.

That's how my only friend is,
not loud, not showy, but always there.

The War Within

I'm not too good at goodbyes,
I always move away from the tearful eyes.
I loathe the weight of parting pain,
The lingering ache that is too heavy to
abstain.
So, one day, I decided to slip away,
Without anyone noticing and without any
farewells.

I'm not too good at speaking right,
So I just watch through the silent night.
They ask me, "What's been going wrong?"
I smile, and say "Nothing," and play along.
But in my mind, a battle is being fought,
An unseen Trojan war of sorts.

I'm not too good at telling lies,
So I try to leave words in plain disguise.
I make it tres light, I make it tres small,
To ease their hearts, I often take it all.
For what they bear, I bear it too,
An untold pact they'll never know.

Old Cardigan

I had a cardigan, rich in color,
soft against my skin, just the right warmth.
But one day, as I leaned against a bench,
an iron nail tore through the sleeve.

Frustrated, I stitched it back,
hoping it would last forever.
It didn't.
A few more wears, and it unraveled,
beyond repair, beyond saving.

I searched everywhere
markets, stores, endless pages online
but nothing matched.
Not the color, not the feel,
not the way it once made me feel.

A year passed, and I found another,
different, but still special.
I wore it on quiet evenings,
on days that felt like they needed something
extra.
But time worked against it too.

The fabric lost its glow,
the softness faded,
and no amount of care could bring it back.
I still wore it,
but without the same admiration.

Things that once felt irreplaceable
become familiar,
and familiarity makes us forget
how much we once loved them.

Art Never Comes First

They say, "Read science, it's the key,
"Arts is for those with lesser dreams."
They claim that logic shapes our fate,
While passion walks a lesser state.

They're rational, but do they see?
That art holds truths as deep as sea.
Nature hums for those who hear,
And strength survives through more than
fear.

Darwin's words shaped how we evolve,
Yet Keats brought solace to hearts in dreams.
Wordsworth's verse, so soft yet wise,
Still lifts the weary and calms their cries.

The Big Bang told how the universe began,
Yet stories kept the soul of man.
Philosophers like Socrates and Plato with
minds profound,
Without their thoughts, would truth be
found?

Science and art, are a single thread,
Without one half, the other's dead.
Science and art are nothing but,
Two sides of the same coin.

From Paradise to Scorched Skies

In the heart of nature's vast domain,
I wished to be a bot, void of pain.
No warmth to lose, no chill to feel,
A stoic soul made of metal and steel.

But as coldness swept further
My arms were cold yet melting like icebergs
My Emotions were crumbled, my heart was
scared,
A wishful thought that'd turn into despair.

How strange the odds, how fierce the cost,
In dreams of calmness, so much was lost.
An unseen storm, a silent cry,
Brought havoc down from a cloudless sky.

Paws retreat, the wild withdraws,
Nature's strength now fractured and flawed.
Once mighty, now a fragile thread,
A whisper in the concrete woods where a roar
once led.

Oh, Earth, our home, so deeply scarred,
By hands that once revered and marred.
May we restore with humble grace,
The balance lost in our sacred place.

Vampire Smile

November 29th, a cold sunlit day,
Siliguri's air crisp with winter's breath.
A penultimate spot, an admission secured,
Yet time was fleeting, the hills called me back.

Classes would start, but I was unready,
Belongings away, an absence to explain.
Pen in hand, a letter to write,
Beside me, a father guiding his daughter's words.

I watched, amused, at his careful dictation,
Why would she, in her master's years, need his
aid?
A brief exchange, a name, a town,
Then the last bus called, and I was gone.

March 22nd, seasons had shifted,
Yet fate had woven its unseen threads.
A moment shared with a girl of grace,
A smile adorned with vampire teeth.

The rain arrived, yet she did not waver,
No rain check, no retreat, just quiet resolve.
Under one umbrella, a world unfolded,
Stories exchanged, moments recalled.

November 29th, she said with a laugh,
Her father beside her, a letter in hand.
The memory struck like a destined note,
The man I met, the voice I heard was hers.

As they say, when the universe conspires,
Paths intertwine in the most subtle ways.
And so I met her, the girl of quiet strength,
The embodiment of serenity,
The keeper of a smile so contagious,
 so radiant and so unforgettable.

Lupus

You were diagnosed, and it shattered me.
Watching you in pain, helpless,
With your own body unable to tell friend from
foe.
A cruel disease where the body attacks itself,
Turning strength into exhaustion, resilience into a
daily battle.

Relentless Diabetes and unyielding hypertension
A constant struggle, an endless weight.
Yet you cook, you clean, you care for everyone.
But who cares for you?

Being a homemaker is already hard,
With lupus, it becomes the hardest job in the
world.
Still, you carry on, unshaken,
A silent warrior, stronger than anyone knows.

You are my role model,
Not just as a mother, but as a person.
You shaped me with wisdom,
Taught me kindness, resilience, and grace.

You are the strongest woman I've ever known,
And for that, I am endlessly grateful.

Plastic Nostalgia

I once told myself a lie,
And it became my very reality.
That was until Winter came
Crashing down my impenetrable walls
Like a dreary silent storm approaches,
Engulfing everything in it's way,
The hollow seeds of obliviousness,
That I had once purposely let sprout ,
Were now being pulled over with a force oh so
wild.
That which once believed to be bonafide was now
but just a misguide,
That even the mighty tides which were now so
mild,
Couldn't prevent my mind from losing its summer
isle.
The bubble I seeked refuge in burst wide open,
And the lie I told myself was now but just plastic
nostalgia, a lie well dressed in sepia.

Thou Whose Genesis

Thou who brings forth the clustered emotions of
I, to poetry,
Thou whose Genesis sowed the seeds of
uncertainty in my paradise,
Would thee ever know what a mastermind, I
always was?
Would thee ever appreciate the unkindled verses
thou never deciphered?

Neither the blue bird, nor the pink and purple
hexed Glamgram would help unravel,
With spring yet to come, and winter yet to leave,
One fine night as the Gregorian almanac had only
275 nights left to spare,
The Aquamarina shined brighter for thy arrival.

The serene dawn brought forth thee; a non
chalant bee.
An unsung melody of Crimson hovered in the
breeze ever since,
With no one brave enough to take the leap of
faith, thou were solitary delightfully.
But thy fate intertwined with mine had plans of
intervening with stratagem indifferent,
Were thou really alive in the hourglass as the
sands dripped into the column 28 short of half a
ton,
Although Thou remained as inscrutable,
unimpassioned icy cold flames lit from within...

Crimson Cynthia was now a ghost

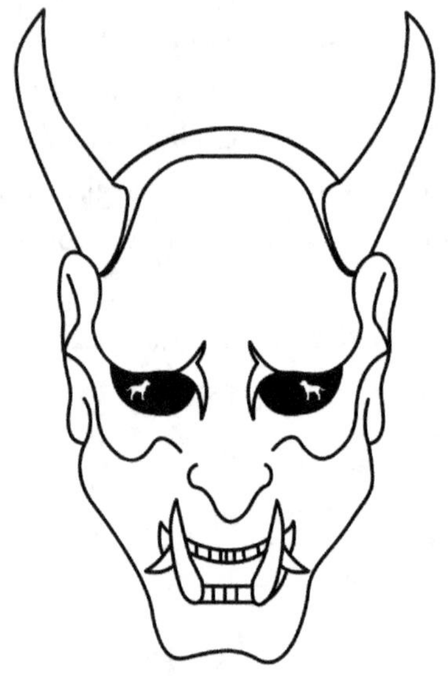

One fine summer day,
It started pouring outta nowhere,
Gloomy skies, misty roads,
Covered in soot,

Crimson Cynthia was now a ghost,
In the veil, she was lost,
A careless child now a cynical adult,
Trying to ascend into the world of angels.

However little did she know,
demons weren't suited for paradise.
Ahh! What a pity, her soul oh so non chalant
Looking for an eternal slumber,
Walked right into a desperate disorder.
Crimson Cynthia was now a ghost.

Seasons of NBU

Where seasons change, so do the moments,
Yet each corner of NBU holds its traces.
November arrives with fall settling in,
Trees stand bare, with whispers of winter on the
horizon.

Brown leaves cover the campus,
Cold wind whispering through the empty paths.
NBU in winter feels calm and endless,
A quiet beauty only the season brings.

Then spring arrives, and colours return.
Near the microbiology department,
The bougainvillea tree reaches its peak,
Pink petals covering the ground like a carpet.

People pause, capturing its beauty,
A moment that never lasts long enough.
Evenings bring another kind of wonder,
From the chemistry ground, the sublime hills
glow,
Kurseong's twinkling lights, Kanchenjunga in full
view.

October makes the little river within come alive,
Framed by wild sugarcane on both sides,
Blessed by the spirit of puja,
It flows with a quiet grace.

Near the rubber plantation, a different scene,
Tall trees stand close, dark and deep,
Their silence holds a mysterious charm.
Passersby stop, drawn to its vintage feel.

The humanities ground hums with energy,
Groups of students sitting, eating, talking,
Some with tea, some with parathas,
Lost in conversations that stretch through the day.

NBU is a place of shifting stories,
With new faces arriving and departing every
season
And around every corner,
a new tale is written all over again.

Ice Cream & Tea

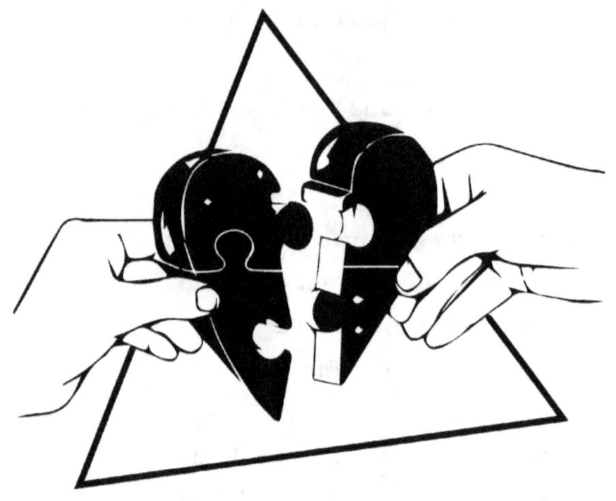

When stress weighs heavy, ice cream is the cure,
A simple joy, a moment of sweetness,
Melting worries with every cold bite,
Bringing happiness, even on the hardest days.

If you quit, who will eat your ice cream then?
Think of the scoops left behind, untouched,
The flavors that never get to dance on your
tongue,
The comfort that never reaches your soul.

If sadness lingers, just grab a scoop,
Let the chill sink in, let it remind you,
Winter is the best time for ice cream.
Some call it a summer treat, but to me,
It's a love that stays, no matter the season.

Tea, however, is eternal.
Seasons may change, but cardamom-ginger milk
tea
That remains, warm and unwavering.
With each sip, spices unfold like colors on a
canvas,
A gentle painting of warmth, scent, and solace.

Flavors swirl, ginger's bite, cardamom's whisper,
Wrapping around my senses, soothing my soul.
Tea and ice cream although opposites in nature,
Yet both, in their own way, bring comfort.

Jorethang Rockstar

I met him by chance in the hills of Darjeeling,
Next door, a voice that set the skies ringing.
From Jorethang he came, with dreams like mine,
But his talents were rare, like aged fine wine.

Heavy metal and rock, were his domain,
His roars like thunder, fierce and untamed.
On stage, he'd summon the wildest crowd,
Heads would bang, and voices loud.

One evening unplanned, with drinks in hand,
Juicy chicken on the plate
Through Darjeeling's roads, he led the way,
To Happy Valley, where memories stay.

Above Lebong, where the cold winds blow,
He strummed his ukulele, soft and slow.
Nepali folk songs filled the air,
Two homesick brothers, lost in a prayer.

Then "Country Roads" we sang as one,
Under the sky, where the sun dipped beyond the
horizon.
Not just a student, but something more,
A singer, an explorer, with talent untold.

Smoking deepened his voice so low,
Yet he knew my limits, let me say no.
Rockstars may be wild, Victorians wise, But he
was the best of both worlds combined.

Ode to a Summer Luncheon

You were the one I shared my lunches with,
Not a friend, not a lover, just company for a meal.
From the hills to the plains,
From the rivers to the lakes,
From the forests to the trenches,
There wasn't a place you didn't fancy.

"Shall we go out tomorrow? Are you free?"
"Yes, of course, but maybe over the weekend?"
Perfect.
What began as casual outings
Turned into quiet, familiar rituals,
A rhythm of plans made and plans undone.

Then life shifted, schedules tangled,
Conversations faded into silence.
No more distant rides, no more shared tables,
Yet, of all the people I've dined with,
None as often as you.

I have no idea where you are now,
Or if someone else braves the extra spicy foods
you loved,
But I hope your lunches are slow and unhurried,
And that, somewhere, you still savour the taste of
those afternoons.

One Rupee Coin

When a one rupee coin is placed with care on a
gift.
It's more than just a coin, it carries a deeper
meaning.
It's a quiet blessing, a part of Shagun,
A wish for something new to begin.

One is whole, unbroken, complete.
In Hinduism, zero marks an end,
But one signifies a fresh start,
A reminder that good wishes
Should never be divided, never fade.

Tradition weaves it into moments that matter,
A silent thread between giver and receiver.
A small gesture, yet filled with intent,
Carrying hope from one hand to another.

And so this poem, the last in these pages,
Sits here like that coin, left behind with purpose.
A wish for you, dear reader,
For luck, for light, for all that lies ahead.

Note from the Author

Dear Readers,

Thank you for having the patience to read my poetry till the end. This has been a journey we've covered together, every word, every verse, a shared stream of consciousness. When you read my poems, in a way, you live through them with me.

I hope my poetry gives you courage, helps you find your voice, and reminds you that you're not alone. Whenever life feels overwhelming, speak up. Talk to someone close, let your emotions flow, and never let silence weigh you down. For me, poetry has always been an outlet, a place where I could pour my thoughts when words felt too heavy to speak. Sometimes, I wrote in diaries, other times, in poems. I've been writing since I was 13. Now, 10 years later, I've finally realized my dream of having a book of my own.

Whatever you carry in your heart, let it out. Writing, speaking, creating art whatever form it takes, it will lighten the weight on your soul. The more you hold in, the harder it gets. Be kind to yourself. Take care.

Much love,
Bishal Raj

Email: bishalrajbiswas@gmail.com
Instagram ID: @bishalrajbiswaz